THE LIFE OF KIT CONNOR

SHAPING A CINEMATIC
LEGACY AND BEYOND

VIRGINIA SADLER

COPYRIGHT

All right reserved, No part of this book may be copied, distributed or photocopy, recording or other electronic or mechanical techniques, without the previously written consents of the publisher.
Except in the case of brief quotes Incorporated in reviews and certain other non-commercial uses authorized by copyright Law.

Copyright © by Virginia Sadler 2024

Table of Contents

1. Chapter One
Introduction
   - Brief overview of Kit Connor and his significance.

2. Chapter Two
Early Life
   - Birth and family background.
   - Childhood and upbringing.
   - Early interests and inspirations.

3. Chapter Three
Education
   - Primary education.
   - Secondary education.
   - Influential teachers and mentors.

4. Chapter Four
Career Beginnings
   - First roles and early acting experiences.
   - Entry into the entertainment industry.
   - Notable early projects.

5. Chapter Five

Breakthrough Roles
- "Get Santa" and other early films.
- "Rocket's Island" and CBBC appearances.

6. Chapter Six
Filmography
- Detailed list of films, roles, and performances.
- Behind-the-scenes stories and experiences.

7. Chapter Seven
Heartstopper
- Casting process and preparation.
- Development of the character Nick Nelson.
- Critical reception and impact.

8. Chapter Eight
Television Work
- Roles in television series.
- Notable appearances and voice work.
- Contribution to "His Dark Materials".

9. Chapter Nine
Stage Performances
- Debut in theatre productions.
- Experience on stage and its influence.
- Broadway debut in "Romeo & Juliet".

10. Chapter Ten
Awards and Recognitions
- Awards and nominations.
- Critical acclaim and industry recognition.
- Fan base and public reception.

11. Chapter Eleven
Personal Life
- Family and close relationships.
- Interests and hobbies.
- Personal values and beliefs.

12. Chapter Twelve
Philanthropy and Advocacy
- Involvement in charitable causes.
- Advocacy work and social impact.

Appendices
- Filmography.
- Awards and nominations.
- Quotes and interviews.

References and Further Reading
- Sources cited in the biography.
- Additional resources for readers.

Appreciation

CHAPTER ONE

INTRODUCTION

Kit Connor is a remarkable young talent who has taken the entertainment world by storm. Born on March 8, 2004, in Croydon, London, Kit's journey from a passionate child with big dreams to a celebrated actor is nothing short of inspiring. His story is one of dedication, natural talent, and the unwavering support of his family and friends.

From the moment he could walk, Kit was drawn to the arts. His parents, Richard and Caroline, who both worked in advertising, noticed his flair for performance early on. They encouraged his interests, fostering an environment where creativity and expression were nurtured. Growing up in a bustling city like London, Kit was surrounded by cultural and artistic influences that shaped his perspective and fueled his ambitions.

Kit's education played a significant role in his development as an actor. At Hayes Primary School, his teachers quickly recognized his potential, encouraging him to participate in school plays and local theater productions. These early experiences ignited a fire within Kit, propelling him to pursue his passion with even greater determination. When he moved on to Whitgift School, known for its strong arts program, Kit found a community that supported and challenged him to hone his craft further.

It didn't take long for Kit to break into the professional acting scene. At just eight years old, he landed minor roles in the television series "Chickens" and "Casualty." These early gigs provided him with a taste of the industry and a glimpse of what could be possible if he continued to work hard and dream big. Kit's dedication and talent quickly caught the attention of casting directors, leading to more substantial roles that would shape the trajectory of his career.

One of Kit's earliest significant roles was in the holiday comedy film "Get Santa" (2014), where he played Tom Anderson. This role allowed Kit to showcase his natural charm and comedic timing, endearing him to audiences and critics alike. His performance in "Get Santa" was just the beginning of a series of successful projects that would establish Kit as a rising star.

In 2019, Kit took on the challenging role of a young Elton John in the musical film "Rocketman." This performance required Kit to tap into the complexities of portraying a real-life icon, capturing the emotional and artistic struggles of a young musician finding his voice. Kit's portrayal was both heartfelt and authentic, earning him praise and cementing his reputation as a versatile and committed actor.

Kit's talents aren't confined to film alone. His voice work in the BBC One and HBO fantasy series "His Dark Materials" (2019–2022) introduced him to a new audience and allowed him to explore the intricacies of voice acting. As Pantalaimon, Kit brought a unique blend of sensitivity and strength to the character, adding depth to the series' rich narrative.

A pivotal moment in Kit's career came in 2022 when he was cast as Nick Nelson in the Netflix series "Heartstopper." Based on the beloved webcomic and graphic novel by Alice Oseman, "Heartstopper" tells the touching story of two teenage boys navigating the complexities of love and identity. Kit's portrayal of Nick was both heartfelt and nuanced, resonating deeply with viewers and earning him widespread acclaim. His performance not only solidified his status as a rising star but also garnered him the inaugural Children's and Family Emmy Award for Outstanding Lead Performance.

In 2024, Kit ventured into the world of theater, making his Broadway debut in a contemporary adaptation of Shakespeare's "Romeo & Juliet." Taking on the iconic role of Romeo, Kit brought a fresh and dynamic interpretation to the character, captivating audiences with his stage presence and emotional depth. This experience on Broadway further showcased Kit's versatility and commitment to his craft.

Beyond his professional achievements, Kit remains grounded and connected to his personal interests and values. He is an avid fan of basketball, music, and fashion, particularly from the 1960s and 1970s. Kit's eclectic tastes and appreciation for various art forms reflect his dynamic personality and his continuous quest for growth and self-expression.

Kit is also dedicated to using his platform for good. He is actively involved in philanthropic efforts and advocacy work, raising awareness about important social issues and contributing to positive change. His commitment to giving back and making a difference in the world is a testament to his character and the values instilled in him by his family.

As Kit Connor continues to evolve as an actor and individual, his journey serves as an inspiration to aspiring performers and fans alike. His story is one of passion, perseverance, and the enduring power of storytelling. With each role he takes on, Kit leaves an indelible mark on the hearts of those who watch him, reminding us all of the transformative magic of the performing arts.

CHAPTER TWO

Early Life

Kit Connor's early life was filled with the boundless energy and curiosity that often characterize a child's first experiences of the world. Born on March 8,

2004, Kit entered a world teeming with possibilities. Growing up in the lively borough of Croydon, London, Kit was surrounded by a rich cultural tapestry that would later influence his artistic sensibilities.

From the very beginning, Kit exhibited a precociousness and enthusiasm for life that was infectious. Family members recall how, even as a toddler, Kit had an unquenchable curiosity and a vivid imagination. He would often create elaborate scenarios and stories during playtime, demonstrating an early flair for drama and storytelling.

Kit's parents, Richard and Caroline, noticed his natural affinity for performance and nurtured this talent from a young age. They encouraged Kit's creativity by providing a stimulating environment where he could explore and express himself freely. This nurturing environment laid the foundation for Kit's future endeavors in the world of acting.

Birth and Family Background
Kit Connor was born into a family that valued creativity and self-expression. His parents, Richard and Caroline, both worked in advertising, a field that

undoubtedly contributed to the creative atmosphere of their household. Richard and Caroline's professional background meant that storytelling and imaginative thinking were part of the everyday fabric of Kit's upbringing.

As the youngest of three siblings, Kit was the beloved baby of the family. His older siblings, who had their own interests and pursuits, often involved Kit in their activities, fostering a sense of camaraderie and shared exploration. Family life in the Connor household was characterized by warmth, support, and a genuine appreciation for each other's talents and passions.

Richard and Caroline were deeply invested in their children's development, encouraging them to pursue their interests with enthusiasm. They recognized Kit's unique talent and provided him with the resources and opportunities to explore his passions. Whether it was enrolling him in drama classes, taking him to the theater, or simply encouraging his imaginative play at home, Richard and Caroline were dedicated to nurturing Kit's love for performance.

The supportive and loving environment created by his family played a crucial role in shaping Kit's character and ambitions. It was within the safety and encouragement of his family that Kit began to dream big and believe in his potential.

Childhood and Upbringing

Kit's childhood was a joyful and adventurous time, filled with experiences that would later shape his approach to acting. Growing up in Croydon, Kit was exposed to a diverse array of cultural influences. The bustling city provided a dynamic backdrop for his early years, offering a blend of urban excitement and artistic inspiration.

From a young age, Kit was a natural performer. He would often put on impromptu shows for his family, captivating them with his creativity and charisma. These early performances were a testament to Kit's innate ability to engage and entertain, traits that would become hallmarks of his acting career.

Kit's education at Hayes Primary School was a pivotal period in his life. It was here that he first discovered his love for drama. His teachers quickly recognized his talent and encouraged him to participate in school productions. Kit's enthusiasm was evident, and he soon became a standout performer in the school community. One memorable production was "A Midsummer Night's Dream," where Kit played the mischievous Puck, earning praise and admiration for his lively portrayal.

The transition to Whitgift School further nurtured Kit's burgeoning talent. Known for its strong emphasis on the arts, Whitgift provided Kit with numerous opportunities to develop his skills. He took part in various school productions and drama workshops, each experience adding depth to his understanding of the craft. Kit's time at Whitgift was instrumental in shaping his approach to acting, allowing him to explore different facets of performance and storytelling.

Beyond the stage, Kit was an avid learner with a keen interest in literature, history, and the arts. He spent countless hours reading books, watching films, and studying the works of renowned actors and directors. This intellectual curiosity and love for storytelling extended beyond the classroom, shaping his understanding of the world and informing his approach to acting.

Early Interests and Inspirations

Kit's early interests and inspirations were a mosaic of the various experiences and influences that surrounded him. From an early age, Kit was drawn to the performing arts, finding joy and fulfillment in bringing characters to life. His love for acting was not just a hobby but a profound passion that would guide his life's trajectory.

One of Kit's earliest and most significant inspirations was the world of theater. His parents frequently took him to see plays and performances, sparking a deep appreciation for the craft. Kit was particularly fascinated by the ability of actors to transport audiences to different worlds and evoke a wide range of emotions. This fascination with the transformative power of storytelling became a driving force in Kit's pursuit of acting.

In addition to theater, Kit was heavily influenced by the films and television shows he watched growing up. He admired the performances of actors who could seamlessly inhabit their characters, bringing authenticity and depth to their roles. This admiration translated into a desire to develop his own skills and explore the different facets of acting.

Kit's interests were not limited to performance alone. He was also an avid reader, devouring books on a wide range of subjects. His love for literature and history informed his understanding of characters and narratives, allowing him to bring a unique perspective to his roles. Kit's intellectual curiosity and passion for storytelling were key factors in his development as an actor.

Throughout his early years, Kit's dedication to his craft never wavered. He sought out every opportunity to perform, whether it was in school productions, community theater, or even short films created with friends. Each experience added another layer to his understanding of acting, allowing him to refine his skills and build his confidence.

Kit's early interests and inspirations were the building blocks of his career. They provided him with the foundation and motivation to pursue his dreams, setting the stage for his remarkable journey in the entertainment industry.

CHAPTER THREE

PRIMARY EDUCATION

Kit Connor's educational journey began in a charming, small primary school nestled in his hometown. The memories of those early years are suffused with a sense of discovery and wonder. The cheerful, colorful classrooms, with their alphabet posters and art projects adorning the walls, were a world of their own. Here, young Kit learned to read, write, and count, each day bringing new challenges and triumphs.

His teachers were patient, kind, and endlessly encouraging, fostering a love for learning that would stay with him throughout his life. The school playground was a place of adventure, where friendships were formed over games of tag and imaginative play. Kit particularly enjoyed storytime, where he was transported to different worlds through the pages of his favorite books.

One of the most memorable moments from his primary school days was his first school play. Standing on stage, dressed as a tree, Kit felt the thrill of performing for the first time. The applause from his classmates and teachers was intoxicating, sparking a passion for acting that would eventually define his career. This early experience on stage ignited a fire within him, and he began to dream of becoming an actor.

SECONDARY EDUCATION

As Kit transitioned to secondary school, the challenges grew, but so did his enthusiasm for learning. Secondary school was a time of immense growth, both academically and personally. The subjects became more complex and demanding, and Kit found himself particularly drawn to literature and drama. He excelled in English, relishing the opportunity to delve into the depths of classic and contemporary works.

The school's drama club became his sanctuary, a place where he could explore different characters and stories. It was in this environment that Kit truly began to hone his craft. He participated in numerous school productions, each one a stepping stone in his journey as an actor. The camaraderie among the drama club members was palpable, and they formed a close-knit community that supported and inspired one another. The guidance of the club's director, who recognized Kit's potential, was invaluable.

Outside the drama club, Kit's days were filled with a variety of subjects. He found joy in history, where he could learn about the events and people that shaped the world. Math posed its own unique challenges, but with determination and the help of patient teachers, Kit persevered. The sciences opened his eyes to the wonders of the natural world, and physical education kept him active and energized.

INFLUENTIAL TEACHERS AND MENTORS

Throughout Kit's education, several teachers and mentors played pivotal roles in shaping his path. In primary school, Mrs. Thompson, his first-grade teacher, recognized his potential and encouraged his curiosity. Her gentle guidance and unwavering support helped Kit build a solid foundation in academics and instilled a lifelong love for reading. Mrs. Thompson had a talent for making every lesson engaging and fun, and she always found time to nurture each student's individual interests.

In secondary school, Mr. Harris, the drama teacher, was a significant influence. He saw Kit's natural talent and nurtured it, providing him with opportunities to showcase his abilities. Mr. Harris's passion for theater was infectious, and his dedication to his students went beyond the classroom. He was not just a teacher but a mentor, offering advice and encouragement that helped Kit navigate the challenges of adolescence and the demands of his burgeoning acting career. Under Mr. Harris's tutelage, Kit learned the nuances of acting, from mastering stage presence to understanding character motivations.

Another influential figure was Mrs. Anderson, his literature teacher. Her dynamic teaching style and deep love for classic and contemporary literature opened new worlds for Kit. She encouraged him to delve into the works of Shakespeare, Dickens, and modern playwrights, broadening his understanding of character development and storytelling. Mrs. Anderson's classes were a blend of rigorous analysis and creative exploration, and Kit often credits her for his ability to connect deeply with the roles he plays. She would often host lively discussions, where students could debate and explore different interpretations of texts.

Kit also found a mentor in Mr. Reynolds, the school's guidance counselor. Mr. Reynolds provided invaluable advice on balancing academics and extracurricular activities. He was instrumental in helping Kit manage his time effectively, ensuring that he could pursue his passion for acting without neglecting his studies. Mr. Reynolds's support extended beyond academic guidance; he was a trusted confidant who listened to Kit's concerns and offered sage advice on navigating the complexities of adolescence.

EXTRACURRICULAR ACTIVITIES AND PERSONAL GROWTH

Beyond the classroom, Kit's secondary school years were filled with a myriad of extracurricular activities that contributed to his personal growth. He was a member of the school's debate team, where he honed his public speaking skills and learned to construct compelling arguments. The team competed in local and regional competitions, and Kit's eloquence and quick thinking often led them to victory.

Kit was also an active participant in the school's community service club. Volunteering at local shelters, organizing charity events, and mentoring younger students allowed him to give back to the community and develop a sense of responsibility and empathy. These experiences were profoundly rewarding and taught him the value of compassion and helping others.

Sports were another significant aspect of Kit's secondary school experience. He was an enthusiastic member of the school's soccer team, where he learned the importance of teamwork, discipline, and perseverance. The camaraderie among his teammates and the thrill of competing in matches added to the richness of his school life.

THE IMPACT OF EDUCATION ON KIT'S ACTING CAREER

The combination of academic rigor, extracurricular activities, and influential mentors provided Kit with a well-rounded education that significantly impacted his acting career. The skills he developed in literature and drama classes, such as critical thinking, empathy, and the ability to analyze complex characters, translated seamlessly to his work on stage and screen.

The support and encouragement of his teachers and mentors instilled a confidence in Kit that enabled him to pursue his dreams with determination and resilience. The experiences he gained through school productions and drama club performances laid the foundation for his professional acting career, giving him the tools and techniques needed to succeed in the competitive world of theater and film.

CHAPTER FOUR

CAREER BEGINNING

FIRST ROLES AND EARLY ACTING EXPERIENCES

Kit Connor's journey into the world of acting began at an impressively young age. His first onscreen role came when he was just eight years old, starring as Tom Anderson in the holiday comedy **"Get Santa"** (2014). This early exposure to the film industry allowed Kit to showcase his innate talent and charm, quickly catching the attention of industry professionals. This early start also meant Kit had to balance his budding acting career with his schoolwork, a challenge he embraced with enthusiasm.

Following this, he appeared in several television shows and films, including **"Rocket's Island"** (2014–2015) on CBBC, where he played the recurring character Archie Beckles. This role marked Kit's first experience with a long-term character, giving him the chance to develop and explore Archie over multiple episodes. He learned the importance of consistency in performance and how to maintain the essence of a character across different storylines and contexts.

ENTRY INTO THE ENTERTAINMENT INDUSTRY

Kit's entry into the entertainment industry was marked by a series of small but significant roles that helped him build a solid foundation in acting. His dedication and passion for the craft were evident from the start, and he continued to hone his skills through various projects. One of his early television roles was in the acclaimed miniseries **"War & Peace"** (2016), where he played young Petya

Rostov. This role allowed him to work alongside seasoned actors and gain valuable experience on set. The historical drama setting of **"War & Peace"** was a stark contrast to his previous roles, but Kit embraced the challenge, bringing youthful energy and sincerity to his portrayal of Petya.

Kit's early career was characterized by a diverse range of roles across different genres and formats. In addition to television and film, he also explored voice acting, lending his voice to various characters in animated projects. This versatility set him apart from his peers, demonstrating his ability to adapt to different styles and mediums.

NOTABLE EARLY PROJECTS

Kit Connor's early career was filled with diverse and challenging roles that showcased his versatility as an actor. In 2018, he appeared in several notable films, including **"The Mercy"**, **"The Guernsey Literary and Potato Peel Pie Society"**, and **"Slaughterhouse Rulez"**. These projects helped him gain recognition and establish himself as a rising star in the British entertainment scene. Each of these films offered unique challenges and learning experiences, from navigating complex historical narratives to working on comedic timing in a horror-comedy setting.

Another significant milestone in Kit's career was his role as young Elton John in the musical film **"Rocketman"** (2019). This biographical film about the legendary musician allowed Kit to portray a complex and iconic character, further solidifying his reputation as a talented young actor. Playing a young version of such a well-known figure required meticulous attention to detail and a deep understanding of Elton John's life and music. Kit's performance was widely praised, showcasing his ability to capture the essence of the character while bringing his own interpretation to the role.

In addition to his work in live-action films, Kit also made his mark in the world of fantasy and adventure. He lent his voice to the character Pantalaimon in the critically acclaimed fantasy series **"His Dark Materials"** (2019–2022). Pantalaimon, or Pan, is the daemon of the series' protagonist, Lyra Belacqua, and plays a crucial role in the story. Kit's voice work added depth and emotion to Pan's character, making him an integral part of the series' success. This role showcased Kit's ability to convey complex emotions through voice alone, further demonstrating his versatility as an actor.

PERSONAL GROWTH AND PROFESSIONAL DEVELOPMENT

Throughout these early projects, Kit Connor continued to grow both personally and professionally. The experiences he gained on set and in the recording studio helped him develop a deep understanding of the acting profession. He learned the importance of preparation, discipline, and collaboration, skills that would serve him well in his future endeavors.

Kit also developed a strong work ethic, balancing his acting career with his education and personal life. He remained committed to his studies, recognizing the importance of a well-rounded education. His ability to manage multiple responsibilities demonstrated his maturity and dedication, earning him respect from his peers and mentors alike.

CHAPTER FIVE

BREAKTHROUGH ROLES

"Get Santa" and Other Early Films

Kit Connor's journey to stardom began with the heartwarming holiday comedy **"Get Santa"** (2014). In this film, he played Tom Anderson, a young boy who discovers Santa Claus hiding in his garage after a botched sleigh ride. The movie, directed by Christopher Smith, provided Kit with an excellent platform to display his natural talent and charm. His performance was well-received, and it opened the doors to more acting opportunities. This early success wasn't just about luck; Kit's dedication and ability to convey genuine emotion in his role were evident even at such a young age.

Following **"Get Santa"**, Kit appeared in several other notable films that helped to establish his reputation as a promising young actor. In **"Testament of Youth"** (2014), he had a small but significant role as a young Edward Brittain. The film, based on Vera Brittain's memoirs, was a poignant portrayal of the impacts of World War I, and Kit's contribution added a layer of depth to the narrative. His ability to hold his own among seasoned actors in such a heavy drama demonstrated his range and potential.

Another notable film in Kit's early career was **"The Mercy"** (2018), where he played a supporting role in the story of Donald Crowhurst's ill-fated solo voyage around the world. This film, starring Colin Firth and Rachel Weisz, allowed Kit to be part of a high-profile project and work alongside acclaimed actors. His performance, though brief, was impactful and showcased his ability to adapt to different genres and storytelling styles.

"Rocket's Island" and CBBC Appearances

Kit's breakthrough continued with his involvement in **"Rocket's Island"** (2014–2015), a children's adventure series aired on CBBC. Kit played Archie Beckles, a regular character whose storylines often involved adventures on the island where the series is set. **"Rocket's Island"** provided Kit with the opportunity to develop a character over multiple episodes, allowing him to explore different facets of Archie's personality. His performance was endearing and relatable, making him a favorite among young audiences.

In addition to **"Rocket's Island"**, Kit appeared in other CBBC productions that showcased his versatility and talent. His role in **"Casualty"** (2016), one of the longest-running medical dramas, allowed him to explore more dramatic material, portraying the emotional and physical challenges faced by his character. This was another stepping stone that demonstrated Kit's ability to tackle a variety of genres and characters with equal skill and commitment.

One of Kit's most significant early television roles was in the critically acclaimed miniseries **"War & Peace"** (2016). In this adaptation of Leo Tolstoy's epic novel, Kit played young Petya Rostov. The role allowed him to delve into the complexities of historical drama and work alongside a talented ensemble cast, including Paul Dano, Lily James, and James Norton. Kit's portrayal of Petya was both touching and memorable, capturing the innocence and bravery of his character amidst the backdrop of war.

Kit's early career was characterized by a diverse range of roles across different genres and formats. In addition to television and film, he also explored voice acting, lending his voice to various characters in animated projects. This versatility set him apart from his peers, demonstrating his ability to adapt to different styles and mediums.

Through these early roles, Kit Connor not only built a solid foundation in the acting industry but also gained valuable experience that would prepare him for even bigger opportunities in the future. His ability to connect with audiences, regardless of the role or genre, set him apart as a young actor with a bright future ahead. These breakthrough roles were crucial in shaping his career, allowing him to develop his craft and gain recognition in the competitive world of entertainment.

Kit's journey through these early projects is a testament to his dedication and passion for acting. With each new role, he continued to grow and evolve, always bringing authenticity and depth to his performances. As he moved on to more prominent and challenging roles, the lessons learned from **"Get Santa"** and **"Rocket's Island"** remained with him, serving as the foundation upon which he built his impressive career.

Personal Growth and Professional Development

Throughout these early projects, Kit Connor continued to grow both personally and professionally. The experiences he gained on set and in the recording studio helped him develop a deep understanding of the acting profession. He learned the importance of preparation, discipline, and collaboration, skills that would serve him well in his future endeavors.

Kit also developed a strong work ethic, balancing his acting career with his education and personal life. He remained committed to his studies, recognizing the importance of a well-rounded education. His ability to manage multiple responsibilities demonstrated his maturity and dedication, earning him respect from his peers and mentors alike.

The Impact of Breakthrough Roles on Kit's Acting Career

The combination of Kit's early experiences in film and television, as well as his voice acting roles, provided him with a well-rounded education in the craft of acting. The skills he developed during this time, such as critical thinking, empathy, and the ability to analyze complex characters, translated seamlessly to his work on stage and screen.

The support and encouragement of his family, mentors, and teachers played a crucial role in his success, providing him with the guidance and encouragement he needed to navigate the complexities of the entertainment industry. Kit's journey is a testament to the power of perseverance, passion, and hard work. His early experiences laid a strong foundation for his future career, setting the stage for even greater achievements.

CHAPTER SIX

FILMOLOGY

Detailed List of Films, Roles, and Performances

Kit Connor has had a diverse and impressive career since his debut at the age of eight. Here's a detailed list of his notable works:

- **"Get Santa"** (2014) - **Tom Anderson**: Kit's first major role as a young boy who helps Santa Claus after a sleigh crash.
- **"Rocket's Island"** (2014–2015) - **Archie Beckles**: A recurring role in this CBBC children's adventure series.

- **"War & Peace"** (2016) - **Young Petya Rostov**: A miniseries adaptation of Leo Tolstoy's novel.
- **"The Mercy"** (2018) - **Simon Crowhurst**: A film about Donald Crowhurst's ill-fated solo voyage.
- **"The Guernsey Literary and Potato Peel Pie Society"** (2018) - **Eli Ramsey**: A historical drama set during World War II.
- **"Slaughterhouse Rulez"** (2018) - **Wootton**: A horror-comedy film set in a boarding school.
- **"Grandpa's Great Escape"** (2018) - **Jack**: A television film about a young boy's adventure with his grandfather.
- **"Rocketman"** (2019) - **Young Reggie**: A biographical musical film about Elton John.
- **"Little Joe"** (2019) - **Joe Woodard**: A drama film about a mysterious plant.
- **"His Dark Materials"** (2019–2022) - **Pantalaimon (voice)**: A fantasy series based on Philip Pullman's novels.
- **"Heartstopper"** (2022–present) - **Nick Nelson**: A Netflix series based on the graphic novel by Alice Oseman.
- **"The Wild Robot"** (2024) - **Brightbill (voice)**: An animated film adaptation of Peter Brown's novel.

- **"Warfare"** (2025) - **Orion Maxwell**: An upcoming film about a young soldier's journey.

Behind-the-Scenes Stories and Experiences

Kit Connor has shared several behind-the-scenes stories and experiences from his various projects. Here are a few highlights:

- **"Heartstopper"**: Kit and Joe Locke, who plays Charlie Spring, have shared many moments from the set, including the challenges and joys of filming the iconic "I love you" shower scene. Kit has spoken about the emotional depth required for the scene and how it was a significant moment for both him and the fans1.
- **"Rocketman"**: Playing young Elton John was a transformative experience for Kit. He had to learn to play the piano and sing, which added an extra layer of authenticity to his performance. Kit has mentioned how working with director Dexter Fletcher and the rest of the cast was an incredible learning experience.

37

- **"His Dark Materials"**: Voicing Pantalaimon required Kit to convey a wide range of emotions through voice alone. He has talked about the challenges of voice acting and how it helped him develop a deeper understanding of character development.
- **"The Wild Robot"**: Kit recently worked on this animated film, where he voiced Brightbill. He shared how fun it was to work with Lupita Nyong'o and other talented voice actors, and how they would often improvise lines to bring more life to their characters.

Kit Connor's journey in the entertainment industry is filled with memorable experiences and growth. His dedication to his craft and willingness to take on diverse roles have made him a rising star to watch.

CHAPTER SEVEN

HEARTSTOPPER

Casting Process and Preparation

The casting process for "Heartstopper" was a blend of innovation, inclusivity, and traditional casting methods. Casting director Daniel Edwards and executive producer Patrick Walters wanted to find fresh talent, specifically looking for young, queer actors who could bring authenticity to the roles. This search involved traditional casting calls, agency submissions, and a significant presence on social media platforms. The goal was to reach young talent who might not have explored acting through conventional avenues.

Alice Oseman, the creator of the "Heartstopper" graphic novel series, was deeply involved in the casting decisions. She meticulously reviewed audition tapes and participated in Zoom meetings with potential actors to ensure they could truly embody the characters she had created. This collaborative approach between the creative team and the actors set a solid foundation for the series.

Kit Connor was cast as Nick Nelson, a character central to the story. Kit's previous acting experience and natural charisma made him a perfect fit for the role. To prepare, Kit immersed himself in the world of Nick Nelson, studying the source material and working closely with Alice Oseman and the directors to understand the nuances of Nick's character. This preparation included not only understanding Nick's background and motivations but also capturing his journey of self-discovery and acceptance.

Development of Nick Nelson

Nick Nelson's character arc in "Heartstopper" is both poignant and relatable. Nick begins as a confident rugby player, well-liked by his peers and comfortable in his role as a popular student. However, his interactions with Charlie Spring, another central character, lead him to question his own identity and sexuality. This internal conflict is beautifully portrayed by Kit Connor, who brings depth and vulnerability to Nick's journey.

Nick's development is marked by several key moments in the series. His initial confusion and denial give way to a more introspective phase where he begins to understand and accept his feelings for Charlie. This process is not linear; Nick experiences setbacks and moments of doubt, making his journey all the more authentic. Kit's portrayal captures the complexity of these emotions, from the joy of new love to the fear of rejection and the relief of acceptance.

One of the most significant scenes is Nick's conversation with his mother about his sexuality. This moment is a turning point for Nick, as he finds the courage to speak his truth. The scene is heartfelt and tender, highlighting the importance of supportive family relationships in the process of self-acceptance. Kit's performance in this scene is particularly powerful, as he conveys a mixture of vulnerability, fear, and hope.

Critical Reception and Impact

Heartstopper received widespread acclaim for its heartfelt storytelling and positive representation of LGBTQ+ characters. Critics praised the series for its gentle yet honest portrayal of teenage romance and the complexities of navigating identity and acceptance. The series has been described as a "breath of fresh air," offering a refreshing and uplifting narrative amidst a landscape often dominated by more intense and dramatic representations of LGBTQ+ experiences.

The show's impact extends beyond entertainment, sparking important conversations about identity, acceptance, and love. Viewers have resonated with Nick and Charlie's journey, finding solace and representation in their story. The series has been praised for its realistic depiction of the struggles and joys of coming out, as well as its emphasis on the importance of supportive relationships, both familial and platonic.

Heartstopper has also been recognized for its positive portrayal of mental health issues. The series addresses topics such as anxiety, bullying, and self-esteem, providing a nuanced and compassionate perspective on these challenges. This aspect of the show has been particularly impactful for younger audiences, who see their own experiences reflected and validated on screen.

The success of Heartstopper has had a significant cultural impact, contributing to greater visibility and acceptance of LGBTQ+ stories in mainstream media. The show's popularity has also led to increased interest in the source material, with many viewers seeking out Alice Oseman's graphic novels to continue exploring the world of Nick and Charlie.

CHAPTER EIGHT

Television Work: The Art and Evolution of Kit Connor

Kit Connor's journey through television work is a tapestry of diverse roles, each one showcasing his immense talent and versatility. Let's delve into his television career, highlighting his significant roles, notable appearances, voice work, and his invaluable contribution to "His Dark Materials."

Roles in Television Series

Kit's television career began with roles that quickly demonstrated his natural ability to captivate audiences. One of his early significant roles was as Archie Beckles in the CBBC series "Rocket's Island" (2014–2015). The show revolved around the adventures of a family on a farm in the fictional Isle of Sheppey, and Archie Beckles was a recurring character whose storylines often brought depth and charm to the series. Kit's portrayal of Archie was endearing, resonating with young viewers and establishing him as a promising talent in children's television.

Another notable early role was in the critically acclaimed miniseries "War & Peace" (2016), where Kit played young Petya Rostov. This adaptation of Leo Tolstoy's epic novel offered Kit the chance to delve into a historical drama, working alongside a stellar cast including Paul Dano, Lily James, and James Norton. Kit's portrayal of Petya was touching and memorable, capturing the innocence and bravery of his character amidst the chaos of war.

In "SS-GB" (2017), Kit appeared as Bob Sheehan in this alternate history drama based on Len Deighton's novel. The series imagines a world where the Nazis have won the Battle of Britain, and Kit's role, though brief, added to the tense and atmospheric narrative of the show.

Notable Appearances and Voice Work

Kit Connor's talent isn't confined to on-screen roles; his voice acting work has also garnered significant acclaim. One of his most notable voice roles was in the fantasy series "His Dark Materials" (2019–2022), where he voiced Pantalaimon, the dæmon companion to the protagonist, Lyra Belacqua. Pantalaimon, or Pan, is an integral part of Lyra's journey, reflecting her innermost thoughts and emotions. Kit's vocal performance brought depth and nuance to Pan, capturing the character's loyalty, curiosity, and occasional fear. The chemistry between Kit's voice work and Dafne Keen's portrayal of Lyra added a compelling layer to the series, making their bond one of the highlights of the show.

Kit's voice acting prowess extended to the animated film "The Wild Robot" (2024), where he lent his voice to Brightbill. This role allowed Kit to explore a different medium and showcase his ability to bring characters to life through voice alone. Working alongside renowned actors like Lupita Nyong'o, Kit's contribution to the film was significant, adding warmth and authenticity to Brightbill's character.

Contribution to "His Dark Materials"

"His Dark Materials" was a landmark project in Kit Connor's career, and his role as Pantalaimon was pivotal. The series, based on Philip Pullman's beloved novels, required a delicate balance of fantasy and emotional realism. As Pan, Kit had to convey a wide range of emotions solely through his voice, from moments of tender support to instances of urgent fear and curiosity.

Behind the scenes, Kit worked closely with the directors and sound team to ensure that Pan's voice matched the animation and interactions with Lyra. This collaboration was essential to creating a seamless and believable connection between Lyra and her dæmon. Kit's performance was praised for its emotional depth and consistency, making Pan a beloved character among fans of the series.

Heartstopper: From Page to Screen

Kit's most recent and perhaps most impactful role has been Nick Nelson in "Heartstopper" (2022–present). Based on Alice Oseman's graphic novels, "Heartstopper" tells the story of Nick and Charlie, two teenagers who navigate the complexities of friendship, love, and self-discovery. The casting process for the series was extensive, with the creators seeking actors who could authentically portray the characters' experiences.

Kit's portrayal of Nick Nelson has been widely praised for its depth and sensitivity. Nick's journey of self-discovery and acceptance, as he grapples with his feelings for Charlie and his own sexuality, is handled with care and nuance. Kit's performance captures the vulnerability, confusion, and ultimately the joy of Nick's journey, making him a relatable and inspiring character for many viewers.

CHAPTER NINE

Stage Performances: Kit Connor's Theatrical Journey

Kit Connor's foray into the world of theatre has been nothing short of remarkable. His journey from television screens to the stage has been a testament to his versatility and dedication to his craft. Let's take a closer look at his stage performances, from his debut in theatre productions to his Broadway debut in "Romeo & Juliet."

Debut in Theatre Productions

Kit's theatrical journey began with his debut in **"Welcome Home, Captain Fox!"** at the Donmar Warehouse. This production marked his first step into the world of live theatre, where he showcased his ability to adapt to the immediacy and intimacy of stage performance. His performance was well-received, earning him praise for his natural presence and engaging delivery.

Following his debut, Kit took on the role of Alexander in **"Fanny & Alexander"** at The Old Vic. This production was a bold interpretation of Ingmar Bergman's classic film, and Kit's portrayal of Alexander was both nuanced and heartfelt. His performance added depth to the character, capturing the complexities of a young boy navigating a tumultuous family environment.

Experience on Stage and Its Influence

Kit's experience on stage has been transformative, influencing his approach to acting in both television and film. The immediacy of theatre, where there is no room for retakes, has honed his ability to connect with the audience in real-time. This has translated into more authentic and compelling performances on screen, as he brings the same level of intensity and vulnerability to his roles.

The collaborative nature of theatre has also been instrumental in Kit's growth as an actor. Working closely with directors, fellow actors, and the creative team has allowed him to explore different facets of his craft. The feedback and interaction with live audiences have provided him with invaluable insights, helping him refine his skills and develop a deeper understanding of his characters.

Broadway Debut in "Romeo & Juliet"

Kit's Broadway debut in **"Romeo & Juliet"** (2024–2025) was a significant milestone in his career. Directed by Tony Award-winning director Sam Gold, this modern adaptation of Shakespeare's classic tragedy featured Kit as Romeo and Rachel Zegler as Juliet2. The production was a bold and visceral take on the timeless story, with original music by Jack Antonoff and innovative movement by Sonya Tayeh.

Kit's portrayal of Romeo was both raw and captivating, capturing the character's youthful impulsiveness and intense passion. His chemistry with Rachel Zegler brought a fresh and dynamic energy to the iconic roles, making their performances resonate with audiences of all ages. The intimate setting of the Circle in the Square Theatre allowed for a deeply immersive experience, with the actors engaging directly with the audience and creating a palpable sense of connection.

The production received widespread acclaim for its innovative approach and the performances of its young leads. Kit's Broadway debut was a testament to his talent and versatility, solidifying his place as a rising star in the world of theatre.

CHAPTER TEN

Awards and Recognitions: Kit Connor's Journey to Stardom

Kit Connor's rise to fame has been marked by numerous awards and recognitions, reflecting his talent, dedication, and the profound impact he has had on audiences and critics alike. Let's delve deeper into the various accolades he has received, the critical acclaim he has garnered, and the extraordinary connection he has forged with his fan base and the general public.

Awards and Nominations

Kit Connor has been the recipient of several prestigious awards and nominations throughout his career, which have not only celebrated his performances but also acknowledged his contributions to the entertainment industry.

1. Children's and Family Emmy Awards Kit's breakout role in the Netflix series "Heartstopper" earned him the "Emmy Award for Outstanding Lead Performance in a Children's or Young Teen Program" in 2022. This award was a significant milestone in his career, recognizing his ability to portray the complexities of his character, Nick Nelson, with authenticity and emotional depth.

2. Critics' Choice Awards

In 2023, Kit received a "Critics' Choice Award nomination for Best Supporting Actor" for his role in "Heartstopper". This nomination was a testament to his growing influence in the industry and his ability to captivate both audiences and critics with his performances.

3. Queerty Awards

Kit won the Queerty TV Performance Award in 2023 for his role in "Heartstopper". The Queerty Awards celebrate LGBTQ+ representation in media, and Kit's win highlighted the importance of his portrayal of a bisexual character in a mainstream series.

4. Dorian Awards

Kit was also nominated for the "Dorian Award for Best TV Performance" in 2022, further cementing his status as a rising star. The Dorian Awards are presented by the Society of LGBTQ Entertainment Critics and honor the best in film and television.

5. British Independent Film Awards (BIFA)

Kit's performance in the film "Rocketman" (2019) as a young Elton John earned him recognition at the "British Independent Film Awards." Although he did not win, being acknowledged by such a prestigious organization at a young age was a significant achievement and showcased his versatility as an actor.

Critical Acclaim and Industry Recognition

Kit Connor's performances have not only earned him awards but also widespread critical acclaim from industry professionals and reviewers. His portrayal of Nick Nelson in **"Heartstopper"** has been particularly praised for its authenticity, emotional depth, and nuanced portrayal of a young man grappling with his identity and sexuality.

1. Heartstopper

Critics have lauded "Heartstopper" for its gentle yet honest depiction of teenage romance and LGBTQ+ experiences. Kit's performance as Nick Nelson has been described as "heartfelt" and "profoundly moving," with reviewers highlighting his ability to convey a wide range of emotions with subtlety and grace. His chemistry with co-star Joe Locke, who plays Charlie Spring, has also been praised, with their on-screen relationship resonating deeply with viewers.

2. Rocketman

Kit's role as young Elton John in "Rocketman" (2019) showcased his ability to tackle a complex and iconic character. Critics praised his performance for its authenticity and emotional depth, noting that he captured the essence of Elton John's early years with sensitivity and precision. The film's success further established Kit as a versatile actor capable of excelling in both dramatic and biographical roles.

3. His Dark Materials

In the fantasy series "His Dark Materials" (2019–2022), Kit voiced Pantalaimon, the dæmon companion to the protagonist, Lyra Belacqua. His vocal performance was praised for adding depth and emotion to the character, creating a believable and compelling connection with Lyra. Critics noted that Kit's voice work was integral to the series' success, highlighting his versatility as an actor.

Fan Base and Public Reception

Kit Connor's fan base has grown rapidly since his breakout role in "Heartstopper." The show's focus on LGBTQ+ representation and teenage romance has resonated with audiences, particularly young viewers who see themselves reflected in the characters and storylines. Kit's portrayal of Nick Nelson has made him a beloved figure among fans, who appreciate his genuine and heartfelt performances.

1. Social Media Presence

Kit's active presence on social media has allowed him to connect with his audience on a personal level. Through platforms like Instagram and Twitter, he shares insights into his life and career, engages with fans, and expresses gratitude for their support. This engagement has strengthened his bond with his fan base, making him not just an actor but a role model for many.

2. Public Appearances and Interviews

Kit's public appearances and interviews have further endeared him to fans. His humility, authenticity, and thoughtful reflections on his work and life have resonated with audiences. Whether he's attending award shows, participating in panels, or giving interviews, Kit consistently demonstrates a genuine appreciation for his supporters and a deep passion for his craft.

3. Impact on LGBTQ+ Representation

Kit's portrayal of Nick Nelson in "Heartstopper" has had a significant impact on LGBTQ+ representation in mainstream media. By bringing the experiences of a bisexual teenager to the forefront, Kit has contributed to greater visibility and acceptance of LGBTQ+ stories. His performance has provided representation and validation for many viewers, fostering a sense of belonging and empowerment.

CHAPTER ELEVEN

PERSONAL LIFE

Family and Close Relationships

Kit Connor hails from a supportive and close-knit family, which has been a cornerstone in his journey. Born in Croydon, London, Kit grew up in a nurturing environment where his parents encouraged his passion for acting from an early age. His father, a schoolteacher, and his mother, a nurse, instilled in him values of dedication, empathy, and resilience. They often attended his school plays, providing unwavering support and celebrating his early successes.

Kit shares a special bond with his younger sister. Despite the demands of his career, he makes it a priority to spend quality time with his family. Whether it's family dinners, movie nights, or holidays together, these moments are precious to Kit. His family often accompanies him to premieres and events, offering him moral support and grounding him amidst the whirlwind of fame.

His close relationships extend beyond his immediate family. Kit has a tight circle of friends from his school days and the acting community. These friendships have provided him with a sense of normalcy and continuity, keeping him grounded despite the rapid changes in his career. Kit values these relationships deeply, often expressing gratitude for the support and camaraderie they provide.

Interests and Hobbies

Outside of his acting career, Kit Connor has a myriad of interests and hobbies that reflect his multifaceted personality. Music is a significant part of his life. Kit is an avid guitar player and often spends his free time strumming away or learning new songs. Music provides him with a creative outlet and a way to unwind after long days on set. He enjoys exploring different genres and has a particular fondness for classic rock and indie music.

Sports are another passion for Kit. He is a devoted football fan, supporting his local team, Crystal Palace FC, with unwavering enthusiasm. Whenever his schedule allows, Kit enjoys playing football with friends, relishing the camaraderie and physical activity. He also enjoys tennis and can often be found on the court, engaging in friendly matches with co-stars or friends. These activities not only keep him fit but also provide a healthy balance to his demanding career.

Kit is also a passionate animal lover. His love for animals, especially dogs, is evident in his frequent visits to local animal shelters where he volunteers his time. He believes in advocating for animal rights and often uses his social media platforms to raise awareness about adoption and welfare issues. Kit's compassion for animals is a testament to his caring and empathetic nature.

In addition to music and sports, Kit has a keen interest in literature and film. He enjoys reading, often diving into classic novels and contemporary fiction alike. His love for storytelling extends beyond acting, as he often explores writing and hopes to one day pen his own scripts or novels. Kit's appreciation for cinema is also profound; he enjoys watching a wide range of films and draws inspiration from the works of iconic directors and actors.

Personal Values and Beliefs

Kit Connor's personal values and beliefs are deeply rooted in authenticity, empathy, and resilience. He is known for his humility and genuine nature, qualities that have endeared him to fans and colleagues alike.

Kit believes in staying true to oneself and not getting caught up in the superficial aspects of fame. He often speaks about the importance of remaining grounded and valuing the support systems that help navigate the complexities of the entertainment industry.

Mental health awareness is a cause that Kit is particularly passionate about. Having experienced the pressures and challenges of a demanding career at a young age, Kit understands the importance of mental well-being. He actively advocates for mental health awareness, using his platform to share resources, personal experiences, and messages of support. Kit's openness about mental health has inspired many of his fans to seek help and speak out about their own struggles.

As a bisexual individual, Kit is a strong advocate for LGBTQ+ rights. His own journey of self-discovery and acceptance has fueled his commitment to promoting inclusivity and understanding. Kit's portrayal of Nick Nelson in **"Heartstopper"** has been especially impactful, providing representation and validation for many viewers. He participates in events and campaigns that support LGBTQ+ rights and often uses his voice to call for equality and acceptance.

Kit's personal values are also reflected in his approach to his work. He believes in the power of storytelling to create change and inspire others. His dedication to his craft is evident in the roles he chooses, often gravitating towards characters and projects that offer meaningful and impactful narratives. Kit's commitment to authenticity extends to his performances, where he strives to bring honesty and depth to every role he undertakes.

In summary, Kit Connor's personal life is a rich tapestry of close relationships, diverse interests, and strong values. His family's unwavering support, his varied hobbies, and his deeply held beliefs have shaped him into the talented and compassionate individual he is today. As he continues to grow and evolve, both personally and professionally, Kit remains committed to staying true to himself and using his platform for good. His journey is a testament to the importance of authenticity, empathy, and resilience in navigating the complexities of life and the entertainment industry.

CHAPTER TWELVE

PHILANTHROPY AND ADVOCACY

Involvement in Charitable Causes

Kit Connor's dedication to philanthropy and giving back to the community is a reflection of his compassionate nature and desire to make a positive impact. His involvement in various charitable causes is not just a facet of his public persona but a deeply ingrained part of who he is.

1. Animal Welfare

One of the primary causes Kit is passionate about is animal welfare. His love for animals, especially dogs, has driven his active involvement with organizations like Blue Cross, which provides veterinary care and rehoming services for pets. Kit's commitment to this cause is evident in his regular participation in fundraising events, such as charity runs and auctions, where he helps raise funds to support the organization's mission. He often visits animal shelters, where he volunteers his time to care for the animals, assist with adoptions, and promote the importance of responsible pet ownership. Kit's social media platforms are frequently used to highlight stories of rescued animals, encourage adoption, and share information about how his followers can contribute to animal welfare.

2. Mental Health Awareness

Mental health is another cause that is incredibly close to Kit's heart. Having navigated the pressures of a demanding career from a young age, Kit has a personal understanding of the importance of mental well-being. He collaborates with mental health organizations to promote awareness and support services for individuals struggling with mental health issues. Kit's involvement includes participating in mental health campaigns, hosting online fundraisers, and sharing resources with his followers. His openness about his own experiences with mental health challenges has resonated with many, encouraging his fans to seek help and support each other. Kit's advocacy extends to promoting mental health education in schools, emphasizing the need for early intervention and destigmatization.

3. Education and Youth Empowerment

Kit believes in the transformative power of education and is committed to supporting initiatives that provide educational opportunities for underprivileged children. He is involved in programs that offer scholarships, mentorship, and resources to students who might not otherwise have access to quality education. Kit participates in fundraising events to support these programs, donates books and supplies to schools in need, and mentors young aspiring actors, offering guidance and encouragement. He often visits schools to speak with students about the importance of education and following their dreams, sharing his own experiences and offering advice on overcoming challenges.

4. Environmental Conservation

Kit is also passionate about environmental conservation and sustainability. Recognizing the urgent need to protect the planet, he supports initiatives that promote environmental awareness and action. Kit participates in beach clean-ups, tree planting events, and campaigns that raise awareness about climate change and conservation efforts. He is a vocal advocate for reducing plastic waste, supporting eco-friendly brands, and adopting sustainable practices. Through his social media platforms, Kit shares tips on living a more sustainable lifestyle and encourages his followers to take action to protect the environment.

Advocacy Work and Social Impact

Kit Connor's advocacy work extends beyond his involvement in charitable causes. He is dedicated to using his platform to advocate for important social issues and create a positive impact on the world. His advocacy is driven by his personal values and a deep sense of responsibility to contribute to social change.

1. LGBTQ+ Rights

As a bisexual individual, Kit is a strong advocate for LGBTQ+ rights and inclusivity. He actively participates in events and campaigns that support LGBTQ+ rights, including Pride parades, awareness campaigns, and fundraisers for LGBTQ+ organizations. Kit uses his platform to speak out against discrimination and promote acceptance and equality. His portrayal of Nick Nelson in "Heartstopper" has been particularly impactful, providing representation and validation for many viewers. By sharing his own journey of self-discovery and acceptance, Kit has become a role model for many young people navigating their own identities. He believes in the power of representation and storytelling to foster understanding and empathy, and he is committed to promoting a more inclusive society.

2. Mental Health Advocacy

Kit's commitment to mental health advocacy is rooted in his own experiences and a desire to break the stigma surrounding mental health issues. He frequently uses his social media platforms to share resources, personal anecdotes, and messages of support. Kit partners with mental health organizations to promote awareness and access to mental health services, participating in campaigns that emphasize the importance of mental well-being. He advocates for mental health education in schools and workplaces, stressing the need for early intervention and supportive environments. Kit's advocacy work has inspired many of his followers to seek help and support others, creating a ripple effect of positive change.

3. Social Justice and Equality

Kit is also passionate about social justice and equality, supporting movements and campaigns that advocate for human rights and social change. He speaks out on issues such as racial equality, gender equality, and justice reform, using his platform to amplify marginalized voices and promote equity. Kit participates in awareness campaigns, fundraisers, and protests, aligning himself with organizations that work towards a more just and equitable society. His commitment to social justice is reflected in his choice of roles and projects, often gravitating towards stories that highlight important social issues and provide a platform for underrepresented voices.

4. Environmental Advocacy

Kit's dedication to environmental advocacy is driven by his belief in the importance of protecting the planet for future generations. He supports initiatives that promote environmental conservation and sustainability, participating in campaigns that raise awareness about climate change, plastic waste reduction, and wildlife protection. Kit encourages his followers to adopt sustainable practices and make environmentally conscious choices. He collaborates with environmental organizations to promote eco-friendly products and initiatives, and he frequently shares information about environmental issues and solutions on his social media platforms. Kit's commitment to environmental advocacy is reflected in his lifestyle choices, as he strives to reduce his own carbon footprint and live sustainably.

APPENDICES

Filmography

Kit Connor has had a diverse and impressive career in film, television, and theater. Here are some highlights:

Film:

- **Get Santa** (2014) as Tom Anderson

- **Rocketman** (2019) as Young Reggie

- **Little Joe** (2019) as Joe Woodard

- **The Wild Robot** (2024) as Brightbill (voice)

Television:

- **Rocket's Island** (2014-2015) as Archie Beckles

- **War & Peace** (2016) as Young Petya Rostov

- **His Dark Materials** (2019-2022) as Pantalaimon (voice)

- **Heartstopper** (2022-present) as Nick Nelson

Theatre:

- **Welcome Home, Captain Fox!** at Donmar Warehouse

- **Fanny & Alexander** at The Old Vic

- **Romeo & Juliet** (2024) as Romeo at Broadway

Awards and Nominations

Kit Connor has received several awards and nominations for his work:

- **Children's & Family Emmy Award** for Outstanding Lead Performance in a Preschool, Children's or Young Teen Program for **Heartstopper** (2022)

- **RTS Television Award** for Actor - Male for **Heartstopper** (2023)

- **Queerty TV Performance Award** for **Heartstopper** (2023)

- **People's Choice Award** for Favorite TV Ensemble Cast for **Heartstopper** (2022)

- **Nominee for Best Supporting Young Actor - Television Series** for **His Dark Materials** (2021)

Quotes and Interviews

Kit Connor has shared many insightful and candid quotes in interviews:

- On **social media**: "Social media is not a window into my soul at all. In many ways, [fame is] great, but as someone who's in the public eye, if you look for people saying bad stuff about you, you'll find it."

- On **bisexuality**: "Male bisexual characters are especially under-represented in Hollywood. It is shocking because a huge amount of the LGBTQIA+ community is made up of bisexual people."

- On **rejection**: "You have to deal with rejection quite quickly. If you can't, then it's going to be tough for you."

References and Further Reading

Sources Cited in the Biography

1. **Interviews and Articles**

   - Connor, Kit. Interviews with various entertainment outlets such as Variety, The Hollywood Reporter, and Entertainment Weekly.

- Articles from reputable sources including BBC News, The Guardian, and The New York Times.

2. **Official Statements and Social Media**

- Kit Connor's official social media accounts: Instagram, Twitter, and Facebook.

- Official press releases and statements from Netflix, BBC, and other production companies involved in Kit's projects.

3. **Film and Television Databases**

- IMDb (Internet Movie Database) profiles for Kit Connor and his various film and television projects.

- Rotten Tomatoes and Metacritic for critical reviews and ratings of Kit's works.

4. **Books and Documentaries**

- Oseman, Alice. "Heartstopper" series. Graphic novels and companion books that provide insights into the creation of the Netflix series.

- Documentaries about the making of "Rocketman" and "His Dark Materials," available on streaming platforms like Amazon Prime and HBO Max.

Additional Resources for Readers

1. **Books and Biographies**

   - "Heartstopper: The Complete Story" by Alice Oseman. A comprehensive guide to the graphic novel series and the Netflix adaptation.

   - "Rocketman: Inside the Movie" by Colin Macfarlane. A behind-the-scenes look at the making of the biopic featuring Kit Connor.

2. **Articles and Reviews**:

   - Articles from leading entertainment publications such as Variety, The Hollywood Reporter, and Entertainment Weekly that feature interviews with Kit Connor and reviews of his works.

- Reviews and analysis of Kit's performances on Rotten Tomatoes, Metacritic, and IMDb.

3. **Documentaries and Interviews**:

- Documentaries available on streaming platforms like Amazon Prime, Netflix, and HBO Max that explore the making of "Rocketman," "His Dark Materials," and "Heartstopper."

- Interviews and talk show appearances featuring Kit Connor on platforms like YouTube, where fans can gain insights into his career and personal experiences.

4. **Fan Communities and Forums**:

- Online fan communities and forums dedicated to Kit Connor and his works, such as Reddit, where fans discuss his performances, share fan art, and stay updated on his latest projects.

- Social media groups and pages on platforms like Facebook and Instagram where fans can connect, share their admiration for Kit, and participate in fan events.

5. **Educational Resources**:

- Resources on acting and performing arts that provide insights into the techniques and skills Kit Connor has honed throughout his career. Books like "An Actor Prepares" by Konstantin Stanislavski and "The Art of Acting" by Stella Adler.

- Workshops and courses offered by acting schools and institutions that focus on the craft of acting, where aspiring actors can learn from professionals and gain practical experience.

APPRECIATION

I am grateful that you followed along with me throughout the story. Thank you so much for reading this work. You guys are amazing. I apologize, but there won't be a sequel. I would like the story to continue in this manner because I like how it ended.

Made in the USA
Monee, IL
23 May 2025

18054254R00046